# ON THE RUN
## True Stories of Legendary Outlaws

# The Story of
# BUTCH CASSIDY
# AND THE SUNDANCE KID

### LINDSEY LOWE

## Enslow
### PUBLISHING

Published in 2024 by Enslow Publishing, LLC
2544 Clinton Street
Buffalo, NY 14224

Portions of this work were originally authored by Tim Cooke and published as *Butch Cassidy*.
All new material this edition authored by Lindsey Lowe.

Children's Publisher: Anne O'Daly
Design Manager: Keith Davis
Designer: Lynne Ross
Picture Manager: Sophie Mortimer

Manufactured in the United States of America

CPSIA compliance information: Batch #CSENS24: For further information contact
Enslow Publishing LLC, New York, New York at 1-800-398-2504.

Please visit our website, www.enslowpublishing.com. For a free color catalog of all our high-quality books,
call toll free 1-800-398-2504 or fax 1-877-980-4454.

Cataloging-in-Publication Data

Names: Lowe, Lindsey.
Title: The story of Butch Cassidy and the Sundance Kid / Lindsey Lowe.
Description: New York: Enslow Publishing, 2024. | Series: On the run: true stories of legendary outlaws |
Includes glossary and index.
Identifiers: ISBN 9781978536715 (pbk.) | ISBN 9781978536722 (library bound) | ISBN 9781978536739 (ebook)
Subjects: Cassidy, Butch, 1866—Juvenile literature. | Sundance Kid—Juvenile literature. | Outlaws—West
(U.S.)—Biography—Juvenile literature.| Crime—West (U.S.)—Biography—Juvenile literature.
Classification: LCC F595.C362C66 2024 | 364.1552092—dc23

Picture Credits
Front Cover: Library of Congress.
Alamy: Room the Agency 15; Johathan Blair: 40; Daily Graphic: 6; Esmoraca & Mojinete Bolivia: 38; Getty
Images: Patrick Bennett/Corbis 35, Denver Post 39, Underwood Archives 27; Paul Hermans: 20; Jerrye and
Roy Klotz: 14; Karen Jensen: 8; Library of Congress: 4, 11, 12, 16, 19, 21, 22, 24, 25, 28, 29, 32, 36, 44; Kim
MacQuarrie: 41; Robert Hunt Library: 13, 45; Shutterstock: 34, John Pablo Bueno 37, Everett Historical 17,
Mariuz S. Jurgielewicz 18, Marzolino 5, Meunierd 23, Lincoln Rogers 31, Joseph Sohm 30 sunsinger 33, Vlad
Turchenko 7; Topfoto: 10, 42; Twentieth Century Fox: 43;
Barbara Whitney: 9.

All other artwork/maps Brown Bear Books

Find us on

# CONTENTS

# INTRODUCTION

Butch Cassidy led the Wild Bunch, one of the most feared gangs of the West. They were famous for robbing banks and trains.

Mormon settlers traveled west to Utah to escape hostility from people in the east. Mormon beliefs had made them unpopular.

The Wild Bunch stole from banks, railroads, and mining companies. Butch said he never shot anyone. Some people admired him. They saw him as an outlaw standing up for the rights of individuals against big business. Butch Cassidy's real name was Robert Leroy Parker. He was born in Beaver, Utah, on April 13, 1866. Utah had only been settled by white Americans about 20 years earlier. It was still part of the frontier.

# A Mormon upbringing

Life in Utah was hard. There was little law and order. Most settlers in Utah territory were Mormons. They included Robert Leroy Parker's parents. Mormons belong to the Church of Jesus Christ of Latter-day Saints. The church had been founded by Joseph Smith in New York State in 1830. Its teachings included the belief that a man could have more than one wife. Such an unusual belief made Mormons unpopular with non-Mormons. The U.S. government tried to ban the religion, and some Mormons were attacked.

The Mormons built Salt Lake City in the desert of Utah. Conditions there were tough.

Joseph Smith was murdered by a mob in 1844. Two years later, a new leader named Brigham Young led the Mormons west. They wanted to find a place where they could practice their religion free from persecution. They walked thousands of miles across the Plains and through the Rocky Mountains, until they reached the Great Salt Lake Basin in Utah, where they settled. Robert Leroy Parker's grandfather had moved to the United States from England. He became a Mormon minister and led his family on the migration westward.

## A hard life

Most Mormon families were farmers. The Great Salt Lake Basin was not suited to farming. The early pioneers had to irrigate, or water, the land to make it suitable for planting crops. However, the community grew quickly.

This cartoon from 1883 shows a Mormon defying Uncle Sam. It poked fun at the Mormons' wish to follow their own laws.

Salt Lake City is still the headquarters of the Mormon faith and the state capital of Utah.

When the Mormons arrived on July 24, 1847, Utah was part of Mexico. The next year, it became part of the United States after the Mexican–American War (1846–48). The Mormons continued to follow their own laws, however. Robert Leroy Parker may not have taken U.S. laws seriously. That may have influenced his later decision to become an outlaw.

# Boyhood In Utah

As a boy, Robert Leroy Parker lived on a small ranch in a remote valley. Life was hard and his father struggled to feed his family.

Robert was the eldest of 13 brothers and sisters. He was known as Bob. He spent the early part of his life in Circleville, Utah, close to what is now Bryce Canyon National Park. He was brought up by his mother, Ann, and his father, Maxi. The family was poor and struggled to support itself.

## Disastrous winter

When Bob was a young boy, his father managed to buy a ranch 12 miles (19 km) from Circleville. The family lived there in a remote two-roomed cabin. Bob worked on the ranch with his father, but they struggled to make a living.

The Parkers moved to this small cabin near Circleville in Utah.

During their first year, bad weather ruined the harvest and a cold winter killed the cattle. Things got even worse after Maxi tried to claim more land. The local Mormon minister gave the land to another homesteader. The 13-year-old Bob and his parents had to find work away from the ranch to earn money. Bob worked on other ranches across western Utah.

## LIKEABLE OUTLAW

Even as a young man, Robert Parker was very popular. He was known for his sense of humor, friendly manner, and charming personality. Such qualities helped him to remain a popular figure even after he became an outlaw.

Utah's landscape was spectacular but it was poor for farming. The Parkers struggled to make a living from it.

# Cowboy Villain

In 1879, Bob Parker met a cowboy named Mike Cassidy. He taught Bob everything he knew, including how to steal cattle and horses.

**B**ob Parker first met Mike Cassidy when they both worked on the same ranch. Cassidy taught the young Bob how to ride a horse, how to shoot a gun, and how to rope, brand, and rustle cattle. By the time he was 16, Bob was said to be the best shot in Circleville. He was also skilled at taming wild horses so they could be ridden.

## Horse thief

Cassidy was also a horse rustler. He took Bob Parker on his raids. At night, the pair stole horses from ranches near the Utah state border. They took the horses over the border. At the time, law enforcement was organized by each state. Lawmen from Utah could not chase them into another state. Cassidy and Parker could sell the horses in another state without fear of being caught.

Mike Cassidy was an expert cowboy. He took Robert Parker under his wing.

Cassidy's first crime was taking a pair of jeans from a store. He is said to have left a note promising to pay for the jeans.

## CATTLE AND HORSE RUSTLING

Stealing horses and cattle was common in the West. Cowboys would steal the animals at night and sell them, often before a rancher had realized they were gone. There was little ranchers could do about it. It was hard to find evidence to catch and prosecute rustlers.

Bob changed his surname to "Cassidy." He changed his first name to George, and later to Butch. There are two stories about how he got the name "Butch." One story says it was because he once worked as a butcher. In the other story, Mike Cassidy had a rifle. He called it "the Butcher" because of its fierce recoil. One day, Bob fired the rifle and was knocked back into a pond. Mike Cassidy gave him the name "Butch" in memory of the occasion!

# Cowboy Life

**Although Butch Cassidy was making a living as a cowboy he wanted more out of life. The work was hard and poorly paid.**

Cowboys moved around to find work. Their job depended on the season. During the winter, they worked on ranches, making sure the cattle did not wander too far. In spring, they rounded up the cattle and rescued cows that had become lost or trapped in bogs. During the summer months, they drove the cattle on long trails to the railroads and to market.

## On the trail

On the cattle trails, cowboys rode all day, slept outside at night, and lived on beef, biscuits, beans, and black coffee. The work was hard. There could

Cowboys gather round the chuck wagon for a meal during the spring cattle roundup.

A cowboy holds his lasso ready to rope any cattle escaping from the herd during a drive in 1902.

be up to 15,000 cattle in a herd, and the herd had to cover an average of 15 miles (24 km) each day. As many as 12 cowboys controlled each herd. They all had to be highly skilled horse riders.

Because their life was so hard, cowboys were usually young. The average age for a cowboy was 24. Like the Native Americans, cowboys were nomads who traveled light. They relied entirely on the cattle for their livelihood and food, as the Native Americans relied on the buffalo.

## DIFFERENT ROLES

Cowboys had different jobs on the trail. The "wrangler" looked after the horses. The "point" rode at the front of the cattle herd. He kept a lookout and turned the herd in the right direction. The "drag" chased up any cattle that fell behind.

# Bank Robbery

Around the age of 18, Butch moved to Colorado. It is thought that he also moved on from rustling to robbery.

On June 14, 1889, four men robbed the San Miguel Valley Bank in the town of Telluride, Colorado. They got away with $20,750. The local newspapers identified two of the robbers as the McCarty brothers, Tom and Bill. Experts now also think this was Butch Cassidy's first bank robbery.

## Outlaw hideouts

The gang had left fresh horses along their getaway route, so they could change horses as they went. This helped them outrun the tired horses of the posse that chased them. The robbers fled to a hideout in southeastern Utah named Robber's

The San Miguel Valley Bank building still stands in Telluride. It was robbed by the McCarty gang in 1889.

Robber's Roost was a canyon with caves and lookout points. Very few outsiders went there, making it a good place for outlaws to hide.

Roost. The hideout was very remote. Law enforcement officials did not even know it existed until after Cassidy's death. Cassidy and his gang used Robber's Roost as a hideout after most of their robberies.

In 1890, Cassidy bought himself a ranch in Dubois, Wyoming. He may have paid for it with the money he had stolen. The ranch was near another isolated hideaway, the Hole-in-the-Wall. Outlaws could hide in the remote canyon for months at a time.

## THE HOLE-IN-THE-WALL

Different gangs used the Hole-in-the-Wall for around 50 years, from the 1860s to 1910. Robbers headed to the remote Wyoming canyon after a robbery to hide from the forces of the law. The outlaws who used it included Butch Cassidy and other members of his gang, the Wild Bunch.

# A Model Prisoner

After buying his ranch, Cassidy continued to rustle cattle and horses. In 1892, the law finally caught up with him.

Butch Cassidy was arrested and charged with stealing a horse. His defense was that he had bought the horse from a rustler without knowing it was stolen. Cassidy was tried at Lander, Wyoming, and found guilty. Long legal delays meant he was not sentenced until 1894. He was given two years in Wyoming's State Penitentiary in Laramie. According to one story, Cassidy asked the local sheriff if he could go home

The state prison in Laramie was intended for Wyoming's most dangerous criminals.

## GETTING AWAY WITH IT

The 18 months Butch Cassidy spent in the penitentiary was the only time the outlaw ever spent in jail. Cassidy was widely suspected of being involved in robbing banks and trains. However, there was never any evidence to allow the law to prosecute him.

This photo of Cassidy was taken in jail. He was prisoner number 187.

for the night if he promised to return the next day. The sheriff was said to have agreed, and also to have lent Cassidy a horse. Cassidy did return, as promised, and began his sentence.

## Planning for the future

After serving 18 months of his sentence, Cassidy wrote to Wyoming's Governor William P. Richards. He asked to be released early. Cassidy had been well behaved, so the governor agreed as long as Cassidy promised to stay out of trouble. However, after his release on January 19, 1896, Cassidy returned to the Hole-in-the-Wall. He was ready to form his own gang and commit more robberies.

# The Wild Bunch

After his release from prison and return to the Hole-in-the-Wall, Cassidy formed a gang with his closest friends.

**B**utch Cassidy's gang included Elzy Lay. They had met when they were both working as ranch hands. The gang also included Harry Longabaugh, who later traveled with Cassidy to South America. Longabaugh's nickname was the Sundance Kid. Some of the other outlaws also had nicknames. Harvey Logan's was Kid Curry.

The number of gang members went up and down. There were around 30 members in all, but most of them were only in the gang for

Winnemucca in Nevada was the scene of one of the Wild Bunch's many robberies in September 1900.

one or two robberies. At least two women also took part in the gang's raids: Laura Bullion and Camilla Hanks.

## Bad reputation

The gang started out mainly robbing banks. Although it was later named the Wild Bunch, the outlaws tried to avoid shooting people. Cassidy claimed that he had never killed anyone.

The gang was at its most active between 1896 and 1901. No one knows how many crimes it carried out, nor how many Cassidy was actually involved in. But the reputation of the Wild Bunch was firmly established. Butch Cassidy and the gang were wanted outlaws with prices on their heads.

## THE SUNDANCE KID

Harry Longabaugh moved to the West with his family in 1881. In 1887, he was jailed for stealing in Sundance, Wyoming. He began to call himself the Sundance Kid. In 1892, he helped to rob a train. Soon afterward, he joined the Wild Bunch.

Jesse Linsley was one of many gang members who took part in Wild Bunch robberies.

# Famous Robberies

The Wild Bunch started off robbing banks. They soon switched to target the mines and railroads of the West to make more money.

On August 13, 1896, the Wild Bunch robbed a bank in Montpelier, Idaho. They got away with $7,000. But Cassidy wanted to make more money. He decided to target the mining companies and railroads. They were better guarded than banks, so robbing them was more risky. Cassidy thought the higher profits made it worth taking the risk.

## Castle Gate

Cassidy usually avoided carrying out crimes in Utah in case someone recognized him, but he made an exception when he targeted the Pleasant Valley Coal Company in Castle Gate, Utah.

Money to pay the miners arrived by train. The company was worried that the train might be robbed. It altered the time the train arrived each day so robbers wouldn't know the timetable.

When the Wild Bunch robbed this bank in Montpelier, a deputy chased them by bicycle.

20

Castle Gate, Utah, was the location of a mine that produced high-quality coal.

Cassidy watched the train arrive every day for a week. Finally, on April 21, 1897, Cassidy and a sidekick—probably Elzy Lay—watched the money being carried off the train in heavy bags. Then they held up the company paymaster, E. L. Carpenter. Carpenter handed over the money, but in the confusion Cassidy's horse ran off. Cassidy had to flee on foot. Nevertheless, he got away with $8,800.

## MINING IN THE WEST

Utah and other states in the West had rich supplies of coal and other minerals. Many companies opened mines to dig minerals out of the ground. The mines were very remote. They relied on railroads to transport the minerals. Railroads also brought money and supplies for the miners.

Cassidy had planned the Castle Gate payroll robbery carefully. He had cut the telegraph wires so Carpenter could not raise the alarm. Cassidy and Lay got away, despite being chased by a posse. They had left fresh horses along their route and knew the land well. That helped them reach Robber's Roost, where they spent the next three months in the hideout.

## Train robbers

Between 1899 and 1901, Cassidy and the Wild Bunch carried out at least five train robberies in Wyoming, Oregon, New Mexico, and Montana. They flagged down a train, then held it up at gunpoint. They always robbed the safe in the mail car, never the passengers. In one train robbery on June 2, 1899, the gang got away with $60,000.

People were fascinated by train robberies. This poster advertised a theatrical performance of a robbery.

## Equal partnerships

The booty from a robbery was always divided fairly. Half went to pay anyone who had helped the gang, such as railroad employees, bank cashiers, or telegraph operators. The other half was divided equally between all members of the Wild Bunch, whatever the size of the part they had played in the robbery.

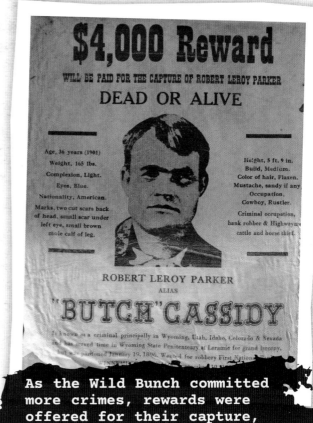

$4,000 Reward

WILL BE PAID FOR THE CAPTURE OF ROBERT LEROY PARKER

DEAD OR ALIVE

Age, 36 years (1901)
Weight, 165 lbs.
Complexion, Light.
Eyes, Blue.
Nationality, American.
Marks, two cut scars back of head, small scar under left eye, small brown mole calf of leg.

Height, 5 ft. 9 in.
Build, Medium.
Color of hair, Flaxen.
Mustache, sandy if any
Occupation,
Cowboy, Rustler.
Criminal occupation,
bank robber & Highwayman
cattle and horse thief.

ROBERT LEROY PARKER
ALIAS

"BUTCH" CASSIDY

Is known as a criminal principally in Wyoming, Utah, Idaho, Colorado & Nevada and has served time in Wyoming State Penitentiary at Laramie for grand larceny, but was pardoned January 19, 1896. Wanted for robbery First National WINNTH.

As the Wild Bunch committed more crimes, rewards were offered for their capture, dead or alive.

## MAJOR WILD BUNCH ROBBERIES

| PLACE | DATE | AMOUNT |
|---|---|---|
| Montpelier, Idaho | August 13, 1896 | $7,165 |
| Castle Gate, Utah | April 21, 1897 | $8,800 |
| Wilcox, Wyoming | June 2, 1899 | $60,000 |
| Folsom, New Mexico | July 11, 1899 | $70,000 |
| Tipton, Wyoming | August 29, 1900 | $55,000 |
| Winnemucca, New Mexico | September 19, 1900 | $32,000 |
| Exeter, Montana | July 3, 1901 | $65,000 |

# The Pinkertons

**Railroad bosses decided to take action. They hired the Pinkerton National Detective Agency to catch the outlaws.**

On June 2, 1899, the Wild Bunch robbed a train near Wilcox, Wyoming. As the gang made its getaway, Sheriff Joe Hazen was shot dead. A group of bankers, businessmen, and railroad owners decided to take action. They hired the Pinkerton National Detective Agency. The agency had first made its name when it had foiled a plot to kill president-elect Abraham Lincoln in 1860.

The Pinkerton agency sent Charlie Siringo to hunt down Butch Cassidy and his gang. Siringo was one of their best agents. He worked with another Pinkerton agent named Tom Horn.

Pinkerton's agents like these traveled on trains in the West to protect them from robbery.

Horn was known to be a killer for hire. Siringo and Horn used different methods to try to locate the Wild Bunch. Horn used threats and violence. Siringo was more crafty. He became friendly with a woman who knew the brother of Kid Curry. Curry was a member of the Wild Bunch.

## A long pursuit

Pinkerton agents pursued Cassidy and his gang for the next 10 years. They collected information about Cassidy, the Sundance Kid, and Sundance's girlfriend, Etta Place. Their information led to the arrest of a number of members of the Wild Bunch. In the end, the Pinkerton agency's determination to catch the outlaws persuaded Butch Cassidy and the Sundance Kid to try to give up their life of crime.

Charlie Siringo posed as an outlaw to get himself close to the Wild Bunch.

## A WORLD FIRST

The Pinkerton detective agency was the first detective agency in the world. It was founded by Scotsman Allan Pinkerton in Chicago in 1850. Its badge was an open eye with the motto "We Never Sleep." By 1869, the Pinkerton agency employed about 10,000 people.

# On the Run

With the Pinkerton agents on his tail, Butch Cassidy realized that the days of the Wild Bunch were numbered. Increasingly, gang members were being arrested and jailed.

Cassidy always claimed that he had never killed a man during a raid. That was not true of other members of the Wild Bunch. The gang robbed a train near Folsom, New Mexico, in July 1899. A posse cornered Elzy Lay, Will Carver, Kid Curry, and Sam Ketchum. In the gunfight that followed, the outlaws killed the sheriff and his deputy. Elzy Lay was wounded but escaped. Sam Ketchum was captured. He died of his wounds in jail.

Five leading members of the Wild Bunch (from left to right): Harry Longabaugh, William Carver, Ben Kilpatrick, Harvey Logan, and Butch Cassidy.

A posse loads horses onto a railcar as they set out in pursuit of the Wild Bunch.

## Second thoughts

Elzy Lay was soon captured. He was found guilty of the killings and sent to jail for life in New Mexico. Lay's capture made Cassidy start to think about whether he should continue his life of crime.

Many different lawmen were closing in on the Wild Bunch. Their usual hideouts were no longer safe. The gang had to keep moving. They required all their survival skills to stay alive. They could not light a fire for fear of being spotted; they could not risk staying too long in one place. The outlaws carried the money from their robberies—but they had nowhere to spend it.

## KID CURRY

After the Folsom robbery, Pinkerton agents chased Kid Curry all the way to Arkansas. He was wanted for 15 murders, but he may have killed twice that many men. According to some stories, his luck finally ran out in 1904 after he robbed a train in Colorado. Wounded during a gunfight, he took his own life rather than go back to jail.

# Plea for a Pardon

When Elzy Lay was arrested in 1899, Cassidy decided it was time to give up his life of crime. He came up with a surprising way of going about it.

In 1900, Cassidy went to see Judge Orlando W. Powers in Utah. He asked the judge to ask Utah's governor, Heber Wells, to grant him an amnesty. In exchange Cassidy would give up crime. When the judge could not help, Cassidy went directly to Heber Wells. He agreed to grant an amnesty as long as Cassidy had never been accused of murder. But when he discovered that Cassidy was wanted for murder he withdrew his offer of amnesty.

Utah governor Heber Wells (far right) meets President Theodore Roosevelt (center) in 1903.

## Close to a deal

Cassidy was not put off. He went back to Judge Powers, who this time decided to help. Powers arranged for Cassidy to meet officials from the Union Pacific Railroad. In exchange for no longer robbing their trains, the

Edward Harriman (right) ran the Union Pacific Railroad. He was ready to make a deal with Cassidy.

railroad company planned to offer Cassidy a job as a train guard. The plan fell through when the railroad officials were delayed by bad weather and were late for the meeting.

Cassidy thought he had been deliberately ignored. After a day of waiting, he left the meeting place. His attempt to give up his life of crime had failed. He decided to carry on robbing trains.

## "FOREVER ON THE DODGE"

Cassidy told Judge Powers he was tired of always hiding from the law. He said, "You'll never know what it means to be forever on the dodge."

# End of the Wild West

By the late 19th century, railroads had opened up the American West. Settlers had arrived and laws were being enforced.

In the old Wild West, people used guns to settle disputes. Now law and order were taking over. Sheriffs enforced laws, but it was difficult for them to protect populations spread over vast areas. People often took the law into their own hands. They formed vigilante groups to fight crime. Associations were formed to solve issues of land ownership. As the railroads spread farther west, they hired their own guards to protect their trains.

## Nowhere to run

For outlaws like the Wild Bunch, the Wild West was disappearing as the 19th century came to a close. Agencies, such as the Pinkerton National Detective Agency, employed dedicated agents. The agents were prepared to go to any lengths to catch outlaws.

State capitols, like that of Nevada in Carson City, were symbols of the arrival of law and order in the West.

Despite the end of the Wild West, Wild West shows remain popular today.

The legal system in the West was improving. Police forces worked in larger towns. They enforced laws against carrying concealed weapons, being drunk in public, or gambling. Frontier marshals enforced laws in small communities. With more judges to try cases, and better jails to hold criminals, it was clear that crime was no longer an easy way to make money in the West.

## LAW AND ORDER

Pinkerton's detective agency was not the only group bringing law and order to the West. Banks and railroads began to use other private detectives. Bounty hunters caught outlaws for bounty, or reward money. Volunteers from the U.S. Cavalry also chased outlaws.

# Escape to Argentina

Pinkerton's detectives had not given up and were still hot on Cassidy's trail. He decided to make a new life in South America.

**B**utch Cassidy had enough money to plan a fresh start away from the West. He and the Sundance Kid met up in New York. The Kid had brought his girlfriend, Etta Place, along. Cassidy adopted the alias Jim Ryan, while Sundance and Etta called themselves Mr. and Mrs. Harry Place.

## Going south

On February 20, 1901, the former outlaws boarded a British steamer. They sailed to Buenos Aires in Argentina. The three then traveled farther south. In 1902, Cassidy, Sundance, and Etta settled on a large piece of land in a remote part of Patagonia, in the far south of Argentina.

The Sundance Kid, photographed with Etta Place before moving to Argentina.

## Borrowed time

For three years, the outlaws lived as ranchers, raising sheep, cattle, and horses. Their Argentine neighbors believed that Cassidy and the Kid were brothers. But the Pinkerton agency had not given up. Agent Frank P. Dimaio traced Cassidy to Argentina. Again, the former outlaws were living on borrowed time.

## SETTLING DOWN

In March 1902, Sundance walked into a bank in Buenos Aires in Argentina. He deposited over $12,000 in cash. On April 2, Cassidy and Sundance applied to settle in Cholila, Argentina. Cassidy had fled about 6,000 miles (9,655 km) from the scenes of his crimes in the American West.

Patagonia is one of the most remote regions in the Americas.

# Return to Crime

It is not known why they returned to their old life of crime, but Butch and Sundance started robbing banks in Argentina and Uruguay.

After three years of living quietly on their ranch, Butch and Sundance gave up their peaceful lives. Why remains a mystery. One theory is that an American named A. P. Field arrived in Cholila to buy cattle. He had been a sheriff in Wyoming and recognized Cassidy. Another story is that they knew Pinkerton's agents were closing in on them.

## Bank raids

On February 14, 1905, robbers held up a bank in Rio Gallegos at the southern tip of Argentina. The criminals were probably Cassidy and

No one knows why the outlaws gave up ranching in Patagonia for a new life in crime.

Sundance, even though the town was 700 miles (1,126 km) south of Cholila. They may have been helped by Kid Curry, who had escaped from jail in 1902. He may have traveled south, although some reports say he had killed himself after a robbery in Colorado in 1904.

In March 1906, Cassidy and the Kid stole $20,000 from a bank in Mercedes in Uruguay. Etta stayed in the street to mind the horses. A third robber might have been Kid Curry. There were other bank raids in Argentina, but the identity of the raiders was never confirmed. However, Butch and Sundance sold their ranch and left Cholila for good.

## MISTAKEN IDENTITY?

Among other crimes, Butch Cassidy and the Sundance Kid were accused of killing a man in Arroyo Pescado, Argentina, in 1910. But there were two problems with the accusation. First, killing was not their style. Second, they are thought to have been dead by then.

The three outlaws left their isolated ranch house in Cholila around summer 1906.

# Going Straight

**After selling the ranch in Cholila, Cassidy and Sundance went their separate ways. But they were not apart for long.**

**S**ometime in 1906, the Sundance Kid returned to the United States with Etta Place. The two traveled to San Francisco. Etta had grown tired of their life in South America, but no one really knows why.

## A new identity

Meanwhile, Butch Cassidy moved across the border from Argentina to Bolivia and renamed himself James "Santiago" Maxwell. He got a job at the Concordia tin mine near the village of Tres

Sundance and Etta Place moved to San Francisco at the time when the city was being rebuilt following an earthquake in April 1906.

The Concordia tin mine was in the foothills of the Andes in Bolivia.

Cruces, 90 miles (145 km) southeast of the Bolivian capital, La Paz. Cassidy quickly became known as an excellent worker. He was put in charge of the mine's payroll.

The Sundance Kid did not remain in the United States for long. The Pinkerton detectives many have been on his trail. He made his way to the tin mine in Concordia. Cassidy got him a job. At the mine, the outlaws became friends with an engineer named Percy Seibert. He would play a crucial role in the final chapter of Butch and Sundance's lives.

## A GOOD WORKER

When Butch Cassidy was not robbing banks or trains, he had a reputation for being a hard worker. He had worked on ranches in the U.S. West as well as later at the mine in Bolivia. His bosses there said he was the best worker they ever had!

# The Final Shootout

According to his friend Percy Seibert, Butch Cassidy carried out one last robbery before reaching a violent end. However, mystery still surrounds his death.

On November 3, 1909, robbers stole the payroll of the Aramayo mine in southern Bolivia. Three days later, two American men arrived in the mining village of San Vicente. They took lodgings in a boarding house. A witness saw that their mule was marked with the brand of the Aramayo mine. He told a Bolivian military patrol about the mule.

## What happened next?

There are different accounts about what happened next. One account is that a soldier entered the house where Cassidy and Sundance

San Vicente today is still a mining settlement high in the Bolivian Andes.

The outlaws were said to have died in the small boarding house where they were staying.

were staying and was shot dead by Cassidy. Two other soldiers opened fire on the house. Meanwhile, the military captain ordered the villagers to surround the building so the fugitives could not escape during the night. In one story, Sundance went outside to grab a rifle but was shot. Cassidy was said to have rescued him, but was also shot. They went back inside. There were screams from the house and then silence.

When the soldiers entered the house the next morning, they found both men dead. From the look of their wounds, it was thought that Cassidy must have killed Sundance before turning his gun on himself.

## FINDING EVIDENCE

After the men were killed, the soldiers found money from the Aramayo mine and a map of Bolivia in their room. A mine officer identified the dead men as the men who had carried out the robbery. But who were they?

# Did They Really Die?

**The bodies of the men were buried in the local cemetery. But were they really Butch Cassidy and the Sundance Kid?**

**N**ewspaper reports about the shootout in Bolivia did not refer to the bandits by name. The dead men were simply listed as "unknown." But at about the same time as the two men were shot in San Vicente, Cassidy and Sundance disappeared. Mail sent to Sundance in 1909 went unanswered.

Years later journalists began to link Butch Cassidy and the Sundance Kid to the shootout in San Vicente. In 1930 Percy Seibert, their friend from the Bolivian tin mine, claimed that he had identified the dead men as Butch and Sundance.

## Other theories

However, since 1908 the identity of the dead robbers has been fiercely debated.

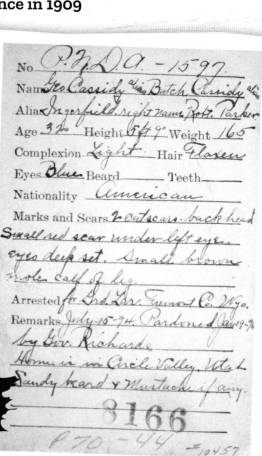

There are few photographs of Butch Cassidy, so identifying the outlaw relied on notes like these.

Author William T. Phillips wrote *The Bandit Invincible*, a life story of Butch Cassidy. Some people claim that he actually was the outlaw.

Some people claim that Seibert falsely identified the dead men in order to give his friends a chance to escape and start a new life. The law officials would stop looking for them if they thought they were dead.

Cassidy's sister, Lula, later claimed that he visited her in 1925. There were other reports of sightings of Cassidy and Sundance across the West long after they were said to be dead. A man named William T. Phillips wrote a book about Cassidy that seemed so accurate some people believed Phillips was really Cassidy.

## UNCERTAIN IDENTITY

No one has photographed the two bodies buried in San Vicente's cemetery. In 1991, the tomb was opened and DNA samples were taken from the remains. The samples only added to the confusion and mystery. They showed that one set of remains belonged to a German miner.

Legacy

The continuing mystery of how Butch and Sundance died has captured the public's imagination ever since.

In the eyes of the law, Cassidy and Sundance were nothing but robbers. However, many people saw them as romantic outlaws. They only stole from institutions such as banks, railroads, and mining companies who could afford it.

## A popular hero

The story that Cassidy and Sundance had died in Bolivia in 1908 began with an interview given by their friend, Percy Seibert, in 1930. In 1975, Cassidy's sister, Lula, claimed that Cassidy had survived and had visited her. With no proof either

Butch Cassidy's sister, Lula, with actors Paul Newman (left) and Robert Redford during the filming of the 1969 movie about Butch and Sundance.

You never met
a pair like Butch
and The Kid

They're Taking Trains...
They're Taking Banks
And They're Taking
One Piece Of Baggage!

20th Century-Fox presents

**PAUL NEWMAN
ROBERT REDFORD
KATHARINE ROSS**

**BUTCH CASSIDY AND THE SUNDANCE KID** ᴬ

A George Roy Hill–Paul Monash Production  Co-Starring STROTHER MARTIN, JEFF COREY, HENRY JONES.
PAUL MONASH         JOHN FOREMAN         GEORGE ROY HILL Written by WILLIAM GOLDMAN
        PANAVISION® COLOUR BY DE LUXE

**The movie was one of the biggest international box-office hits of 1969.**

way, people have made up their own minds about how the pair died—or how they survived.

Books, documentary films, and movies have added to the mystery. The most famous movie was *Butch Cassidy and the Sundance Kid* (1969). It starred Paul Newman (as Cassidy) and Robert Redford (as the Sundance Kid). The movie reinforced the idea that the two men were romantic heroes fighting against the unfeeling capitalism of banks and railroads.

# AN ODD COUPLE

Today people often think of Butch and Sundance together. That is mainly due to the movie *Butch Cassidy and the Sundance Kid*. In reality, Sundance was just another member of the Wild Bunch. Butch was more important, and was the gang's leader.

# Rogues' Gallery

Butch Cassidy had many friends. Most were outlaws and at one time or another took part in the robberies carried out by the Wild Bunch.

### Elzy Lay (1868–1934)

Elzy (born William Ellsworth Lay) was Cassidy's closest friend in the Wild Bunch. He was captured after the Folsom train robbery and sentenced to life imprisonment in New Mexico. After Lay helped put down a prison riot, he was pardoned in 1906. From 1916, he worked as a miner in Wyoming.

### Laura Bullion
### (1876–1961)

One of a small number of women in the Wild Bunch, Laura was nicknamed "Della Rose" by the gang. In 1901, she was convicted of taking part in a train robbery with the Wild Bunch and served three and a half years in jail. After jail, she gave up crime and worked as a seamstress.

## Kid Curry
### (1867–1904?)

Born Harvey Logan, Curry had the reputation of being the "wildest of the Wild Bunch." He had a violent temper, which was made worse when he drank. According to legend, Kid Curry killed at least nine law enforcement officers but he was never charged with murder. He probably took his own life after a holdup in Colorado in 1904.

## Etta Place
### (c.1878–?)

Of all Butch Cassidy's friends and associates, the least is known about Etta Place, Sundance's partner. After she moved to San Francisco in 1906 she disappeared from the records. The only photo that exists of her shows a modest-looking woman. Some people claim she was once a schoolteacher.

## The Sundance Kid
### (1867–1908?)

Born Harry Alonzo Longabaugh in Pennsylvania, he met Cassidy after Cassidy's release from jail in 1896. A member of the Wild Bunch, Longabaugh accompanied Cassidy to South America. The two men lived together with Longabaugh's girlfriend, Etta Place. Some people think he did not die in Bolivia but lived to an old age in Utah.

# Glossary

**Alias** A false identity or name.

**Amnesty** An official pardon for a crime.

**Booty** Valuable stolen goods.

**Capitalism** Economic system in which trade and industry are run by private owners for profit.

**Chuck Wagon** A wagon with cooking facilities providing food on a ranch.

**DNA** A chemical that holds unique genetic information about a person.

**Frontier** The border area between settled land and the wilderness beyond.

**Fugitives** People who are in hiding or who have escaped from the law.

**Hideout** A place used to hide from other people.

**Homesteader** Someone who claims public land to build a home.

**Irrigate** To supply water to crops through artificial channels.

**Migration** The movement of a group of people from one place to another.

**Nomads** People who move around and have no permanent fixed home.

**Payroll** Money used by a company to pay its workers.

**Penitentiary** A prison for people found guilty of serious crimes.

**Posse** A group of citizens helping a sheriff.

**Recoil** The snap back of a gun when it is fired.

**Reputation** How someone or something is judged by the general public.

**Romantic** Associated with an idealized and perfect view of reality.

**Rustle** To round up and steal horses or cattle.

**Theory** A suggested explanation for something.

**Vigilante** Someone who takes responsibility for enforcing the law, even though they have no authority.

# Further Resources

## Books

Bearce, Stephanie. *Awesome, Disgusting Unusual Facts About the Wild West.* Black Rabbit Books, 2024.

Faust, Daniel R. *The Real Story Behind the Wild West .* Rosen Publishing, 2020.

Treadwell, Terry C. *Outlaws of the Wild West.* Pen & Sword Books, 2021.

## Websites

www.eyewitnesstohistory.com/cassidy.htm
An eyewitness account of an 1899 train robbery by the Wild Bunch in Wyoming, written by a mail clerk traveling on the train.

thehistoryjunkie.com/wild-west-timeline/
A timeline of the Wild West from the History Junkie website.

www.utah.com/oldwest/butch_cassidy.htm
Page from Utah.com about the state's most infamous former outlaw. Includes the theory that Cassidy did not die in the final shootout.

www.history.com/news/history-lists/6-things-you-might-not-know-about-butch-cassidy
A History.com page with six surprising facts about Butch Cassidy, including the possible origins of his name.

**Publisher's note to educators and parents:** Our editors have carefully reviewed these websites to ensure that they are suitable for students. Many websites change frequently, however, and we cannot guarantee that a site's future contents will continue to meet our high standards of quality and educational value. Be advised that students should be closely supervised whenever they access the Internet.

# INDEX